51 TIPS FOR THE
NEW OFFICE
EMPLOYEE

A.C. ANTHA

INTRODUCTION

Every office has its own rhythm and way of working, an information flow – for both gossip and work-related information – as well as a decision-making hierarchy that may be very different from the pay-grade/office-size/car-park-closest-to-the-front-door hierarchy.

When you start work in an office, the most important thing you can do is keep your mouth shut and eyes open until you have identified the informal rules and hierarchies. Then, and only then, can you use this knowledge to get ahead.

Crossing the invisible lines of informal office protocols is the fastest way to destroy your chances of promotion. No one will ever tell you what you've done – some may not know or understand because they are unaware that informal rules exist – even though they unwittingly operate within them. But for those who are in the know, when you crossed that line, you proved you haven't the wits to make it in an office environment.

Your career may be permanently stalled within the organization and you may waste years before you realize this fact.

So, here are some tips, in no particular order. Use them, and watch how others use (or fail to) use them. In doing so, you'll find out how the organization really works and give yourself the best chance for success.

1

Never ever cross an Executive Assistant.

They go by many different names depending on the organization – Secretary, Executive Officer, Administrative Assistant – irrespective of title, find out who this person is (there will likely be more than one), who their manager is and give them respect!

Their referent power (i.e. the power they get from working for someone far more important than you) is real. They are the gatekeepers, the bottlenecks and the ones that can make your life misery if you treat them poorly. They have the power to move your work to the top of the priority list ... or to the bottom.

2

Got a problem? Don't complain, don't whinge - no one wants to hear it – they're all too busy.

Yes, the squeaky wheel gets the most grease. But once management realizes they can't fix the wheel?

They throw it out and get a new wheel.

You know what management loves? Solutions ... so if your complaint is valid, package the problem with a cost-effective solution and present it to your manager. That way you are seen as a team player and problem solver, not a complainer.

3

Do the task well.

There is always value in doing a task well – whether it is value for the organization, or value in maintaining your self-respect – no matter how high profile or how basic, menial or tedious a task may be.

Doing a task well will earn you respect and place you in good stead with your manager.

If you can, try to change the way the task is perceived to give it (and you) greater status. Rebranding a task to be of more value to the organization or easier for other contributors to complete can result in a positive rebranding of you.

4

If you aren't asked, don't offer an opinion.

First day on the job? First week? Month? Year?

Unless you're the boss or a specialist of great skill and experience, no one yet sees you as having a worthy opinion on anything!

This will change, but for the time being, keep your mouth shut and eyes open. Trust me, there's nothing more irritating than a new employee sweeping in with confidence and opinions but without a clue. Especially if you have just unwittingly suggested an 'improvement' that has been tried previously, and failed miserably.

Get to know the organization's history first.

5

Hold off on making judgments about your co-workers.

You've just joined the team and whenever someone new arrives in any team, there's a period of adjustment, team dynamics change and resettle – it can take weeks or months.

Sit back and observe - who needs to show off what they know?

Whose knowledge appears substantial initially but then swiftly loses its impressiveness?

Who sits quietly in the corner working hard but actually has all the corporate memory?

Pause. Observe. Then make your mind up about your co-workers.

6

There's always a nutcase.

It's true. There's always someone in any workplace that has to try and turn their day job into a struggle for survival filled with backstabbing and manipulation.

They are small people, who will grasp at any chance to feel powerful.

Minimize your contact with these people.

7

Be professional.

No, we don't care about the boyfriend, the gym, the pets, jewelry and definitely don't air your dirty laundry in the workplace.

Severely limit your discussion on personal matters (to nil) until you have been in a workplace long enough to consider your co-workers more than just colleagues.

Once you become friends, you can share. Before that, you're really just irritating and an emotional drain – big tip - you can tell people have had enough of you when they keep trying to turn away from you to work while you blather on obliviously.

8

Don't stir and don't participate in office politics.

It doesn't do you or anyone else any good.

You think no one noticed it was you stirring? You're wrong. Someone spotted you and while you may never be told to cut it out and grow up, your status as a problem employee will spread and from then on, no matter how good your work, you will always be seen as the less preferred employee.

Ever wondered why some talentless hack was picked for a task over you, even though everyone knows you can run rings around them? Yep, you got spotted. They'd rather have someone else's slow consistency, than manage your problem behavior.

9

And following on from Tip 8 …. Don't make the mistake of thinking it's all about your work. You'd have to be a one-in-a-million genius for it to be all about your work.

If you aren't a genius, then yes, being a nuisance or an irritant in any way will always be a factor in any decision made involving you – whether you are let go from the organization or kept on when times are tight, or promoted … people come to work to work, not to have to manage you because you're precious, fragile or need to be delicately handled, or can't handle yourself professionally around others.

10

Does everyone always say 'yes' to your sterling ideas? Does no one ever argue constructively with you?

You're not that good. No one is that good.

If no one argues with you, or disagrees with you, it's because no one can be bothered. At some stage in the past you've shown you don't pay any attention, won't change your mind, or you are so far off the track in how you think that no one can work out how to bring you back to normal. They just agree because it's easier for them.

They are now biding their time until you leave …

11

If you don't know what you're doing – ask.

There's nothing more irritating than a new employee laboring away in the corner for days only to produce rubbish because they were too embarrassed to ask for direction. Embarrassment is about your ego – and no one but you cares about your ego. Get over it.

You are a new employee. You are expected to ask dumb questions – even the same question more than once.

If your manager gets angry because you're asking questions – then your manager is the problem, not you. Generally, problem managers have been noted by the system – let me guess, they've been doing the same job forever? Gee, I wonder why they haven't been promoted elsewhere.

12

Finished that last task?

Ask for another. Never ever, say you're bored.

Let's be honest, sometimes your manager will be working on a priority task and doesn't have the time to spare to even start you off on something new – acknowledge this aloud to your manager 'I can see you're very busy' and then ask if there's something you can read up on quietly while they finish up their high priority task.

Make allowances. They will appreciate you more for it.

13

Know where you are up to with your tasks and be able to provide a concise report on demand.

There's nothing more terrifying for your manager than losing control of the workload – and that's what having a new employee means. Keep a task list, keep it up to date and put it somewhere your manager can find it.

When you leave the office at the end of the day, deliver a two second update to your manager – but limit your update to comments about the progress of your work, not how good you are at doing it.

14

Save your work where it can be found. No one likes a hoarder.

There's nothing more annoying than having an employee that saves everything on their desktop when there's a shared network drive or an electronic document records management system available for your use.

All it takes is a failure in the desktop back-up system (assuming you have one, many offices don't) to lose all your work ... or worse yet, you take a sick day and someone else has to redo all your work. Way to shine.

15

Be personable and ask questions (not too personal) of other people.

Then listen to the answer.

Most people don't listen to the answer, and certainly don't remember the answer more than a few seconds later. If you can remember what you are told, you will stand out.

Never underestimate the impact of showing an interest in another person.

You may also find that the people with whom you work are far more interesting and multi-dimensional than you had first believed. This will enrich your life - which shouldn't be all about work anyway.

Do not spend the entire conversation looking for an opportunity to wedge in a comment about you – especially when the comment is really about one-upmanship. That behavior belittles those with whom you speak, and they will be less inclined to speak with you further.

Admit it – you know someone who does this all the time! Frustrating, aren't they?

16

Social media is not for the workplace unless it's in your job description. Personal telephone calls and personal business should not occur during working hours even if all your work has been completed to a very high standard.

17

If it's working hours be at work, not sick, not at the shops, not trawling for coffee, not hung over and recovering from a weekend of self-abuse. And don't boast about what you did to make yourself sick and less useful to others at work.

Everyone was young once, most can probably outdo you with their stories, but most have already realized that boasting about killing brain cells or engaging in illegal activities is puerile and amateurish and not appropriate workplace behavior.

18

Never send an email when you're angry.

Type it out, save it, then go back the next day and edit it. If you don't have a day to spare, try and tone it down, or ask someone you trust to review your work. There's always a way to rephrase your writing that's not angry, and not rude, but will still get the message across.

A better option is to make a phone call instead – it takes less time and people are more pliant on the phone than by email, where they have time to misinterpret your response and get angry about it.

You may gain concessions this way, and after you've discussed work, you can casually ask a question or two and try to get to know the person better and improve your working relationship.

Adding a personal touch to the end of a phone call can leave them with a better impression of you.

19

Work isn't a war zone.

It's a place you'll probably go to daily for decades so try to get along, think about how today's actions will impact on you in a year's time and be professional.

This is a workplace, not your personal space, you don't have to have everything your way, you don't have to like everyone, you just have to get the job done and go home.

20

Don't be snippy and definitely don't throw a tantrum – it will mark you forever. Those who witness it will not forget and you will be left with ample time for regrets.

Don't get angry at a low-level powerless person when the one you're really annoyed with is your manager.

Learn to take deep breaths. Keep calm and carry on, while making sure to state your case.

21

Don't take yourself so seriously - no one else does.

They're too busy trying to be taken seriously.

And don't take things personally.

To most people, you only exist peripherally; there are a multitude of more likely causes for their behavior than your existence.

Don't assume you are the center of their world.

22

Don't accept bullying aimed at you or others.

Speak up for yourself and make sure you are treated appropriately.

No one likes a victim – they don't want to be one, and dislike recognizing the signs in others. It is important that you are not perceived as a victim, and for this reason, if bullied, you must speak up, preferably directly to the bully at the time of the incident. You will be surprised at the reaction – most bullies are allowed to get away with their behavior, and don't know how to cope when confronted.

What if someone else is being bullied? This behavior is also unacceptable - but be careful not to take on the role of the protector. Many people live in a constant state of learned helplessness – they are used to other people standing up for them. If you take on the role of the protector they may never learn to stand up for themselves, and worse yet, may drag you into situations specifically so that you can speak on their behalf.

Allow them the privilege of being able to solve their own problems.

23

Whatever has gone wrong today think to yourself 'if this is the biggest problem of my day, then it's a good day.'

You could be making mud bricks by hand in the midday sun for a pittance. Everything could be so much worse. Try and be a little thankful.

And if you can't be thankful, keep it to yourself.

24

Don't worry about how you will achieve things that are far in the future. Get today's work done first.

For large and complex tasks, write a project plan and break down the tasks into manageable chunks.

Feeling overwhelmed?

Write a list of everything you've got on so that you can at least quantify the size of the problem. It may look better than you expect … or much worse, but at least your problem now has a size.

Start carving away at the tasks and crossing them off your list. It is a gratifying feeling and far better than being paralyzed with fear and indecision.

25

Look around, who's doing it right? How? Duplicate.

Don't reinvent the wheel. Remember, your time is their money.

26

Read the manual.

No one wants to explain the obvious to you, not when it has already been handed to you in writing … and especially not when your manager is the person who handed it to you and took the time to write the manual.

If this is the case, acknowledge their work.

Saying thank you is a talent.

27

Know your entitlements as an employee and access them - that's sensible.

But don't trumpet that you've been working the system – that's irritating and mercenary.

28

Give everyone the time of day.

Even if they're more than twice your age and talk slower than all your friends. You may learn something useful about them, the organization or yourself. And almost everyone has something interesting to say.

If you prove that you are open to listening, people will come to you and tell you things you may not otherwise find out.

Information is power – you don't need to use it directly - indirectly can be sufficient, for example, by altering the focus of a presentation from profit (how to make money) to risk (how not to fail to make money).

The information can be essentially the same, but with the right focus, your work will resonate with the right people.

First you need to understand the culture of the organization and its people – this culture is often directed from the top, sometimes unwittingly, and as a new employee it may be some time before you have direct contact with the people at the top – so listen where you can.

29

Be approachable, helpful, but not too compliant.

Yes, provide information when asked, but don't take on too much work. You cease to be helpful to others if the work you do is rushed, late, incomplete or worse still, horribly wrong.

30

Minimize your use of buzz words, especially if you learned the buzz word at college or university – chances are by the time it's in a curriculum or published in a book, the buzzword is already out of date.

Do use buzz words you find online at reputable current websites.

Do keep up to date with newspapers and journal articles relevant to your field, but use this content sparingly – making multiple references to articles will make you sound like a parrot, not an independent thinker.

31

Don't talk or email in chat/internet acronyms such as LMFAO or OMG.

Minimize the use of work-related acronyms in emails also.

32

If it's your mess, confess.

If you are confronted with a mistake of your own making, don't make an excuse – not even a small excuse – no matter how subtle you think you are being, the attempt to pass the buck will be noted. You'll look childish and weak, so instead just man up and take it on the chin. You'll get more respect for that behavior.

If you find your mistake before anyone else, try to fix it - quietly. If that's not possible then just accept you will need to tell your manager and do that within a reasonable time period. Delay is your enemy.

Develop a mitigating strategy to both fix the problem and ensure it can't happen again – by your hand, or anyone else's. Provide this information to your manager when you advise of the situation.

Then you will look like a person of action and your manager will appreciate your extra effort.

Make sure you follow through on your mitigating strategy; making the same mistake twice will make you appear foolish and unreliable.

33

Don't be a joker. Jokers don't get promoted, even if they're great fun to be around and make the working day fly. Too much humor will taint the general impression of you as professional and credible.

34

Leave mess on your desk, but clean up after yourself elsewhere.

Mess on your desk makes you look like you are working, even if it's neatly stacked documents (unless of course the office has a clean/clear desk policy).

Leaving mess in meeting rooms, kitchens or anywhere else just makes you look like a slob. And the task of cleaning often falls to the Executive Assistant – see Tip 1. Your behavior will not be appreciated.

Always carry a note book and pen when you're walking around during work hours, whether to a meeting or to ask someone a question in person – it makes you look busy.

35

Make a blisteringly good first impression. This way, later mistakes are seen as aberrations, not your modus operandi, and are more kindly viewed and more easily forgotten.

If your first impression is an unmitigated disaster, then you may always be seen as a disaster – it is almost impossible to overcome a bad first impression.

36

Find out what the work hours really are – most offices have unspoken rules – for example arriving very early may never be noticed if the office standard is to start at 9:30 a.m. and work back late.

37

Don't hitch your wagon to someone who is heading for the cliff edge or just plain stupid - no matter how important a role they presently fill or how well-connected they appear.

In other words, don't make alliances that will drag you down. Investigate alliances thoroughly as they may be unnecessary or counter-productive.

38

Have a contingency plan – no one works in an office for ever and if the only person who thinks you are excellent leaves the organization, then your status will dramatically change from golden boy/girl to former teacher's pet.

39

Make up your own mind.

People will always be willing to offer you their often uninformed opinion.

Use your own evidence and observations and arrive at your own conclusions.

A truly independent mind is a rarity.

40

Network, including with people with whom you do not need to interact on a regular basis (or at all) to complete your work.

Useful information can come to you by way of networking, and will help you put together the puzzle pieces of the organization's culture. See also Tip 28.

41

Keep your thoughts about other people to yourself.

The last thing you need is to hear your opinion, given confidentially, parroted back to you – whether an accurate rendition, or distorted.

Others will know not to trust you with their information if you can't keep your mouth shut.

42

Accept and value learning opportunities.

Yes, you've probably had your fill of learning by the time you hit the office – whether it is school, college or university.

But note: training opportunities are offered to employees who are seen as worth investing in. This is a good sign!

It is a privilege to be given a training opportunity and to be put in a position that allows you to show you are interested in continuing to improve your skills.

43

Volunteer to be on project teams.

It will expose you to new people, new skills, and broaden your horizons - and it looks good on your resume.

You will be seen by management as a go-getter and not afraid of hard work.

Just make sure to complete the project – many projects get 95% of the way to complete and then just peter out.

The last push is the hardest, but it's where reputations are made.

44

Be a team player.

If someone is struggling in your team, then step up and offer assistance.

However, do not take over unless directed to do so.

45

Dress well – almost as well as your manager.

But don't go overboard – if you're earning $60,000 a year, then a $2,000 suit is taking it way too far.

Dress appropriately for your workplace. If the culture is for conservative dress, then dress conservatively.

If the culture is for crazy individualism – take it as a challenge!

46

Ease up on the visible piercings and tattoos.

Yes, they are more common these days, but a badly placed puncture or unattractively stretched tattoo screams short-sightedness and mediocre decision-making. Especially if you had it done while at university – you must have had an idea of your future career, in which case, what were you thinking? Were you thinking?

47

Did your manager just take credit for your hard work?

Yes it's frustrating, but there really isn't much you can do other than never, ever do that to your own staff in the future.

Trying to take back the kudos through quiet remarks to people will just make you look petty and give the appearance that you are trying to undermine your manager.

Let it go – sooner or later credit-stealers are caught out.

48

So this isn't your first office job?

If you've just shifted from another organization, do not start every sentence with 'Back at XXX, we did it this way!'

It gets tired very fast. Presumably you moved workplaces to get better opportunities and skills. So maybe not everything at your last workplace should be presented as perfect.

49

Don't be resistant when offered new work.

Some people can't help but list all the problems they might encounter with a new task or project – it's their way of managing change. They may not be meaning to sound negative, but it is very tiring for a manager to hear a string of negative comments every time they hand out a task.

Instead, the manager will offer the work to someone else who is more accepting and easier to deal with.

Then you'll be bored, and someone else will be flat out working, and you'll be trying to work out why.

If this is you, or even if you think it isn't, the next time you are offered a new task, try saying 'that sounds interesting, when would you like it completed?' instead and see where it gets you.

Alternatively, you could wait until you are managing one of these people to find out just how annoying it is …

50

Accept and enjoy the differences in people.

In your career you will work with all sorts of people, including those who appear angry and short-tempered, when it's just their way, and no malice is directed at you.

People learn things in different ways - by hearing, seeing or doing. Some like to work with lists and some are incredibly disorganized.

Accommodate these differences. They will enrich your work and private life and make you a better person.

51

Answer the question you are asked.

There are three ways that answering questions go wrong.

The first? You don't read or hear the question properly and so answer the question you think you were asked, or you wanted to be asked, and in doing so, provide irrelevant information ...

Pay attention. If a question is emailed to you, read the email twice – all the way to the bottom of the email – sometimes the most important information is on the last line. Make sure you understand what is being asked. Double check that the email was actually sent to you, rather than you only being copied into the email for your information.

If asked verbally – then speak the question back to the person to make sure you have correctly understood.

The second way ... you give all the information needed to answer the question, but no interpretation and no actual answer.

If all the information you provide in your response is taken from a freely accessible place, such as the office intranet or a manual, then the asker could have found it also. If they've gone to the bother of asking you, then it's probable that they want you to value-add – that is, take the basic information and interpret it in relation to a specific situation detailed in their email. Don't be coy. Give a straight answer.

And, finally, make sure you get the answer is right.

Well, that's my list, based on my experience and observations. It is extensive, but not comprehensive – you will have noticed I skipped over the obvious – don't engage in illegal activities, steal from the organization, gossip, get drunk and dance on tables at the Christmas Party, etc. If you've bought this book, then you have more than enough sense to work those out for yourself.

While much of this seems obvious to me now, it wasn't when I started work in an office – and my many missteps still have the ability to make me cringe.

Hopefully having this information at your fingertips will be of assistance to you and help you avoid some of the pitfalls of office life.

I'd say good luck with your career - but by now you will have realized that luck is just a part of career success.

Planning, self-awareness and understanding are important in positioning yourself to be the right person in the right place at the right time.

Try to enjoy yourself a little too. After all, it's just a job, and over the course of your life, you will find other things that will have far greater value to you.

ABOUT THE AUTHOR

A.C. Antha has more than twenty years' experience working in office environments. She has filled many different roles and worked with a variety of people of different skills, backgrounds and personality types.

A.C. has witnessed (and participated) in a great many strange office behaviors and interactions and it has always been a point of fascination that so many people remain unaware of the unspoken rules.